# Charted Territories

## Astrology in Poetry

Kari Trottier-Whitsitt

Illustrations and Cover Design by Natasha Louie

**BALBOA.**
PRESS
A DIVISION OF HAY HOUSE

Balboa Press books may be ordered through booksellers or by contacting:

Balboa Press
A Division of Hay House
1663 Liberty Drive
Bloomington, IN 47403
www.balboapress.com
1 (877) 407-4847

Print information available on the last page.

ISBN: 978-1-5043-4913-0 (sc)
ISBN: 978-1-5043-4914-7 (e)

Balboa Press rev. date: 02/15/2016

# CONTENTS

# HOUSES
∞

# ELEMENTS
∞

# QUALITIES
∞

# OVERVIEW
∞

Lovingly dedicated to my wife

Wendi

# ACKNOWLEDGEMENTS

I want, first and foremost, to thank my most amazing family: My wife, Wendi Trottier-Whitsitt, my two daughters, Danielle Louie and Natasha Louie, and my son, Cameron Louie for the years of love, support and absolute faith they have in me, and for being my rocks. They are my daily inspiration. I also want to thank my parents, Jerry and Bobbie Whitsitt for their encouragement and love as I pursued this project. A special thank you, again, to Natasha Louie for her wonderful illustrations and book cover design, and for being my kindred muse and crazy brain. I also want to thank my dearest friend, Dianna Gould Brunzell for her steadfast support and encouragement in everything I do, and to Pam Lane for being another pair of eyes and excellent proofreader. A big shout out to Balboa Press — A Division of Hay House for their supportive efforts in actually putting my words into print form, and for the many phone conversations, laughter, and excellent guidance.

Thank you all — My heart community

# INTRODUCTION

I am so excited that you picked up *Charted Territories: Astrology in Poetry*. I am a practicing astrologer of over forty years, and a poet of life. Welcome to my debut book of poetry. There are more waiting in the wings.

I chose to write my first poetry volume, *Charted Territories: Astrology in Poetry,* introducing astrology as a reflection of one and all of us. I became interested in astrology at the age of thirteen and could not get enough of it. The deeper I studied, the more intricately it made sense of the complex nature of personality and human interaction. My emphasis as an astrologer is on personal development and self-discovery. Astrology has opened my eyes to the wonderful interplay of variability within a person and between individuals. It has increased my compassion, understanding and tolerance for the differences that make us unique and which vividly multicolor our world.

I *feel and sense* the psychological art of astrology in images and nuances that lend themselves best in poetic description. Dive into these verses and seek out your very self, for you will find many of your qualities, talents and challenges portrayed in these poems.

Every planet in your birth chart is in a particular astrological sign, including two important luminaries, the Sun and Moon. Therefore, you are an integrated whole of several signs. The houses tell about areas of your life, and also correspond to a particular zodiac sign, as well as being influenced by planets contained in that house. In this volume, you'll find poems for each sign, planet and house, as well as all four elements, Earth, Air, Fire and Water, and the "qualities" (our approach to life) of

Cardinal, Fixed and Mutable. For those new to astrology, I've included a key, located at the end of the book, to all of the above.

Have fun exploring aspects of yourself as you read, and most importantly, *feel*, your way through the pages. Take your time and feast on your own thoughts as you peruse this cosmic spread.

If you need a chart drawn up or a personal reading, printout, or would like to share your thoughts or comments, please contact me at kariwhitsitt@ msn.com. I would be happy to hear from you! Also bookmark my website to keep abreast of future books, speaking engagements, and poetry entries at http://kariwhitsitt.wix.com/the-poet.

# SIGNS

∞

# ARIES

## *Aggressive Innocence*

Curious force of life longing to renew, invent, overtake

The drama and violence of the push

Me first

The sperm shoves past brothers charging headlong into soft things

Desperation of angry howls, unrelenting until the need is met

Taking charge, Crocus forces spring through the snow, and the
first water-filled print turns red on the beach at Normandy

Is it courage, drive, or the fear of ego failing

Intention hints at an answer

Survival instinct of species, youthful exuberance and pioneering,
or thirsty craving for glory, domination, or control

There is an innocence to the compelling nature

Action requires little of forethought

Baby's reach to beautiful blue flame

Some unseen mechanism of initiative, insistent on advancing

Powerful urges make beautiful things or magnificent
destruction, and most likely the juxtaposition of both

Bloody, torn vessel releases the beauty of the newborn

Treasured gems offered in love deny a blasted mountain

Elephants lay wasted in the mud as music vibrates from the tap of ivory

"I" supersedes "you," oblivious of consequence

Shiny, infant pines dot the multi-acred landscape
ravaged by fire — their only means of germination

Burning lava incinerates life as it creates a new land

The itch of drive is the insurance of perpetuation

Spiraling galaxies dance a heated frenzy
toward explosion, and a star is born

The sexy, hot, selfish violence of essential boom

# TAURUS

## *Gluttonous Lover*

Insatiable sensuality

Quivering desire

How can the Earth hold so much beauty

Offerings too vast to resist

The skin must explore

Rough/Smooth — Cold/Hot — Soft/Sharp — Wet/Dry

Ravenous abandon

Wondrous appreciation of life

Green, vivid, tasty jewel of our galaxy

I am your lover

Massage my bare feet as I wriggle my toes into your mud

I close my eyes and embrace the wind and salt spray while sailing your oceans, or lying naked in the sun absorbing pungent mountain pine

My tongue longs for the honey of your bees

Amber drops of sticky sweet

I open my legs to the river's water, and a sigh sounds the ecstasy

Searching the velvet black, your eyes sparkle back
with shining subtle hues of diamonds suspended

Gifts of love given

Mold it all with capable hands

I create

Your seed planted resource within

Build it

Strong, sturdy permanence

Man-made replicas

Useful delight turned greedy desire

Possessive love threatens the sanctity of enough

Numbing excess makes me weep

All magic lost in the tipping point

Soothe my frenzied lust

Extinguish my fire before it destroys your body

Wrap me in comfort and sing me to sleep

Whisper restraint and save us both

My true longing is your pure unadulterated glory

Raw, primitive splendor

Return to simplicity

Kiss me temperate and placid

I am yours

# GEMINI

## *Shallow Brilliance*

White dots dance wildly in the blue sky

Absent of apparent pattern

Quicksilver encounter

"Hello-Goodbye, it's time to fly"

Avoid the sticky paper of emotion where death of freedom is eminent

Linger not or sink you will

Stalled engines plummet, and rocks sink or skip across ponds

Movement essential

Momentum is a cohesion of uplift

The messenger of concentric rings rippling out
gathers knowledge on its way to shore

Dogs smell the intel traveling by wind

Take in the clean and friendly breeze

Open your windows – captured air becomes stagnant

Routine is boredom and carefully uninspiring

Talk me clever

Quip me interested

Beautiful, mental gymnast, swing continuous

Ring to ring, satellite to Earth, sender to receptor

Dots and dashes of meaning at the speed of thought

Depend not

Changes many can happen from acorn to oak, morning
to night, hour to hour, thought to conclusion

Forks in the road are encountered or created

Seeming singularity

Monogamous thought, deed, feeling, or promise

But...cells split, and one are two...or three or four

Be confused or aware of much more

A light heart may keep up, and a sigh of relief
crosses the lips of all others left behind

Inconsistency is the nature of evolution

# CANCER

## *Temperamental Mother*

Heavy, full breasts dripping mana

Gather the hungry in your loving arms

Reciprocal need

Hera — Quan Yin — Mother Mary

Moody moon's silver glow

Pull water through my veins, influence my brain,
wash my shores and collect my flotsam

Round is your form

Belly home of baby

Safe womb of creation

Weepiest of willows

Salt tears of the sea, roll down her face in lunar
rhythm of ever-changing emotion

Never forget

Hoard the memories and please the ghosts

Ancestral influence felt at the touch of Grandmother's tatted lace collar

Attic of antique dreams and cellar's musty
spores carry the seeds of history

We advance, lessons in hand and sins of
our fathers buried deep in DNA

Foundation of basement knowledge

Gather security

Banks and bonds and pantries of food — never to want

Conservative provider

Supply dependency and co-happiness

Needy interchange where fear is satisfied

Safety of locked doors — shell of armor — defensive cage

Avoid pain and skitter sideways, clever crustacean

Snap those crabby claws of beware and self-protective posturing

Iridescent opal of many colors

Oyster's irritation made pearl

Reminisce life's beauty and fill us with unending stories

Of love and betrayal, conquest and peace, feast and famine

We will honor you forward

And ancient hands will touch the face of the future

# LEO

## *Ruling Need*

Deny me not my spotlight nor eclipse my ball of fire

Admiration ignites my soul's expression

Leave me not alone on stage, for there would be no one to warm...
and the flower in my extended hand would drop petals of sadness

Worth is dependent on reception

Useless is the gift unopened

What good is the Sun in an empty universe

In your eyes, I see my radiance reflected
and am inspired to shine brighter

Boldness demands space...and bright colors will be seen

Life is large and loud, and I revel in the boom of my voice

Flair is gleeful, and sequins sparkle my very Joy to the World

Be my subject — I promise to rule justly and lavish you with luxury

To give is how I know to love

Stars supply life to orbiting galaxies

Protons and electrons respect the nucleus

We all aim for the bull's eye

Center holds responsibility, and is the only refuge in a hurricane

The Queen of Hearts must *give* her tarts

To steal them denies her pleasure

Receive with gladness, thank her profoundly...
and you may keep your head

She but wants your love

# VIRGO

## *Discriminative Servant*

Thinly sliced precision and critical angles create a more worthy cog

Tight ships, tight lips, and collars folded just so

Machines run perfectly and hangers on the rod lined
up one inch apart reveal the beauty of order

Research done, analysis speaks current hypothesis
of the right and wrong way to do things

The right and wrong way to live

The right and wrong way to be

Get it right

Tested and tried

Critical discernment

Harsh reality and high expectations you best meet

All casualties stacked neatly in a grave of discarded imperfection

"Every opportunity was given to improve," he pontificates

The loneliness of reason echoes loud in his perfect heart chambers,
and he inches toward knowing the sterility of rightness

Best interest and service the goal, but so few
understand the clarity of exact prisms

The ironclad, no-nonsense exterior conceals the
softer fecundity of good and brilliant intent where a
beating and controlled bleeding heart labors

Labors for you

Due credit is unnecessary

The microbial nutrients of the earth are given freely
and modestly, and the mechanism behind the rainbow
secretly smiles, reveling in the gift others enjoy

Lay down the cruel mirror held to his face

He has intricately inspected his own Petri dish

Unrelenting, self-imposed pressure is the birthing pain of
coal to multi-faceted gem, and self-awareness sparkles
bright knowledge through crystal clear eyes

Pay attention and take no offense while under his microscopic analysis

No one will work more diligently for positive result

Harm nor insult is ever intended; though you may tire as his project

Mental agility made practical — answers are not static info but
dynamic improvement — and a broken body emerges Adonis

Paradoxical soothing of dirt and earth, decaying leaves and
fermenting berries warmed by the sun after rain - all cleanse his soul

Mother Nature's embrace reveals secrets

The interdependent dance where strange and unlikely
beauty is found in the process of becoming

Order come undone — so magnificently necessary

Ahh...sweet respite from straight lines and conformity to exacting
standards — He allows her reality and calms his itch to improve

Offer him a gentle sanctuary

Feed him vegetables of substance and do not
deny him the dessert of your kiss

He is to lead us through a maze of intricate discovery and evolution

Our joy, his reward

# LIBRA

## *Amour a La Tête*

Billowing fabric of sheer azure — welcoming threshold to visual delight

Mastery of Nature's own beauty

Manicured rows, rounds, tiers and strategically placed fountains

Refined aesthetic

Garden retreat, worthy of graceful sensibilities
and symmetry's balance

Softness of petals to soften the heart as water's
music splashes happy off the rocks

Impeccable design

Artistic mind emerging glorious

Cerebral ambrosia

Venusian brain

Tea parties and pleasantries; friendliness waves cordial rhythms

Do not upset such niceties, but stand gently weighted on the fulcrum

Teeter-totter — dangerous uncertainty

Tit-for-tat ensures equality — Log a mental record

Fairness spreadsheet

Balanced Account

The word, "LOVE" — linear, left-brained identifier; Mylar tag

The heart only borrows this insufficient descriptive if asked to speak

Such pleasantly, delightful, lovely loveliness held lofty above the neck

Below the throat's nice words resides an untidy, bloody heart,
fearless and open, reaching instinctually for raw power of
uncontained, uncontrolled, unmanaged, un-named emotion

Oh Beauty, don't you know that jagged rips and nasty scars, broken
pieces and faceted shards of uneven angles hold a whole world
of unimaginable, uncontemplated, sublime appeal and wonder

Crudeness offends the puritanical prettiness of dainty dilatants
with their white-gloved smiles and polite salutations

But patina adds such interest to the shiny copper, and
tarnish reveals the presence of life's oxygen

Mistress of social graces, fear not the depths nor natural disparity

Trust love beyond gentile's safe mask

Show all your colors — muddy mixtures, brilliant jewel tones,
delicious discord of disharmonious hues clashing wildly

Sink your heart into the hot mess of real, and
discover the love you so long for

Then... only then, buff and polish to your mind's content...
just to defile again and again with sordid, sticky,
sour, sweet, pungent, salty, passionate kisses

The counterpoise of authentic and contrived

# SCORPIO

## *Clandestine Phoenix*

Crypt of mysteries unearthed through probing eyes laser's blade

Incognito, herself, allowed none other

A piqued discomfort nudges a possible healing —
terrifying discovery's truths prefer deep tombs

Secrets seem safe but fester the boil

The thorn must rise or infect the whole

Deep, dark waters of teaming life unknown

Diver's awe held spell-bound by translucent
creatures and submerged light shows

Reaching toward beauty, one can be stung or surface a treasure

Embrace death, for death holds life

A pine's seed must burst in flame to germinate

Cremate no longer valid thoughts, habits, dreams and dogma

Birth the new from the bloody caul's served purpose

Regenerate and transform old, useless notions

Stubborn clinging to the rusty anchor will feed the ocean's floor

Life will emerge regardless

Sentiment uninvolved

Dammed watery weight — cubic tons of feeling's powerful push

Masterfully built of iron and concrete — sheer force of will

Do not build below the dam

Best let the water flow its natural course,
lest strength become destruction

Less threatening, moving currents feed happy river
banks and laughter of tumbling rocks.

Willow's roots thrive in the freedom of the gift

Passion merging — tight intertwining

Blood run through blood as a spy's micro camera through your veins

She will know every twitch of your soul's movements

Legendary stealth

Fond of dark glasses and impervious expression

Intimate exchange reciprocated on her terms — her timing

You will know when you feel the hot power of her love that
has infused your being and rests soundly in your heart

She slithers in shadows to hide her scars

They are not your business, but they are deep

Forgiveness would heal many a wound — would that she could

Fire will burn them all away one day

Crisis upon crisis stacks the fuel of impending death and transformation

Bear the heat of her pain, and she may
honor you as witness to her growth

Emerging discovery — hot cinders cooled upon rising

The dark allows her sparks to glow

She requires a strong host of gentle knowing

A fierce Angel

Higher wisdom, unaffected, soothes her torched soul

That she may reach your angelic heights is her hidden desire

Compulsive longing to evolve

Stir the cauldron of your various melding
metals poured molten into the mold

What a beautiful creation made together

From her elevated rung – she begins anew...

# SAGITTARIUS

## *Freedom Pontificated*

Robes and arrows, chessboard and mountain's peak

Knowledge abounds and curiosity launches the mind toward discovery

Freely traveling, Yoda winks and invites you to
sit awhile; his staff positioned ready

Hit the road with wanderlust — seeker of truth

Wisdom sounds in your generous laughter, and the happiness
of your smiling eyes clears all skies to azalea blue

Speak us learned

Your words flow wild — fiery enthusiasm

Waterfall of ideation splashes hard and
blunt on the rocks who listen below

Stone carved malleable by sure and speeding droplets

Momentum and movement essential

Athletic teacher

Challenge our notions and stretch our mental
horizons with games of agility

Playful Centaur — the golden key of knowledge swinging
from your neck highlights your glistening muscles

Strength of energetic living

Unbounded freedom quest

Life's meaning hidden in monastery masonry or the chanting of a priest

Perhaps ceremonial candles flicker a message, or the
philosophy of nature, herself, leads you by the hand

Profess your manifesto and quench your thirst for ever changing verity

Tip your goblet to strangers and refill with a global-infused conception

Full-bodied, deeply rich — a rounder, opulent flavor

Variety is the spice of knowledge, and one-
dimensional thought will never do

You waste not one precious drop of life's experience

Bon voyage jolly preceptor — master of optimism

Life is, indeed, good

# CAPRICORN

## *Inhibited Authoritarian*

Serious leader of black and white definitive

Draw the line and sketch out your exacting plan

Public standing — prestige awaits, and your calculated pause
upon the ladder ensures stability of your next step

Strong fortress walls of castle high

Structure your life solid and sure — risk not
the fool's delight of spontaneity

Security demands thoughtful foresight, and rules
ensure conformity of square corners

Melancholy loner

Your worthiness is your singular question

Hold others at arm's length so they may
objectively behold the proof presented

Would but your constant cloud rain appreciation sweetly upon
your cheeks — seeming aloof indifference could melt away

Righteousness of method; your strong suit

Tell others how it should be done — most efficient course or path

Your authority will reign where imposition is not triggered

Inhibit not your secret, unruly jester — his nonsensical
imagination could expand your kingdom

Careful initiator of steady goals — review gray
areas and add color to your drab world

Allow Sun's rays to pierce through narrow windows
and illuminate your hard-won glory

Lonely at the top — depressing cliché

Let the tower crumble and fall — the pillars
remaining will tell your story

# AQUARIUS

## *Odd Sage*

Brilliant mind of mechanistic science

Take us beyond ordinary conceiving to worlds yet unknown

Futuristic fantasy turned factual and fabricated

Electrical matrix streaming

Indigo child of the universal

Knowing is as simple as breathing — flash insight
inhaled through portholes of cerebral matter

Humanity awaits your lead and gathers support around worthy causes

Original thinker, tap us a new dance to the
rhythm of sparks flying from your feet

Lightning cracks our skies open with jolting realization

Ideas cannot be trapped or pinned, nor those inspiring them

Freedom to roam imagination's creative trailheads
and switchbacks is the eccentric's birthright

Clarity of "ah-ha" stimulates an invention or evolving theory

Temporary reality

Unlike any other — weird, opposing, strange,
curious, bizarre, offbeat soul

Make us uncomfortable

Unorthodox savior to our commonplace,
conformity, and unexceptional familiarity

Tomorrow's ordinary is today's freak-out

Status quo is a short-lived comfort and an unworthy goal

Cow prod the people to collective individuality

Separate, unique paths will cross and connect at crucial intervals

And we will grow together

# PISCES

## *Escape Artist*

The fog and beautiful mystery of nuance delights the crazy brain

Feelings, meaning, color and knowing
permeate the heart of the observer

Exactness is literally lost, and expanded, unbounded awareness
leads to connection of the unexplainable intertwining of the whole

Awareness that hovers in the realm of empty
space, where spirit perhaps resides

She opens her mouth, and baffled expressions
mirror her longing for verbal clarity

Dissolving into the swirling, mystic waters where cerebral
computation is not required for understanding

Loneliness holds her hand

Unquantified energy unseen, unheard, is felt

Beyond bones to soul

Watermark influence

Secret, cohesive bond cradles all

Music speaks without lyrics, and color emotes a particular truth

The eye's language is more exact

Were there no tongues, we'd understand

A piece of every other, she sees wholly

A cacophony of thoughts, feelings, intentions, silent reactions

Suffering shared, too often...too much

Tightly twist the psychic sponge in solitude dripping

Quick escape

Compassion is costly without the shield

Barely here

Alternate reality is a clearer stronghold to sensitive souls

Gravity cannot hold poets and dreamers...and
visionaries will always bleed beyond boundaries

Uncontainable

Aware of silent, empty space between the illusion of matter

They slip through with ease

And the muse dances

# PLANETS

∞

# SUN

## *Soul Shine*

Holy heat and master sustenance of every planet

Core ignition of soul's expression

Individual rays of personality to warm one
another — shine bright the story of Self

Rise each morning and direct me, face-forward, toward the challenge
of the day, throwing shadows of my own particular pattern

Ego's bad rap

It is but a toy I play with

Imagination maneuvers my colorful blocks in any various
manner to manifest a more authentic reality

Who am I

Essential question

Golden glow — my vital source — illuminate the answer

Radiate strength, and color my will its own hue of success

Monogram in lights

Marquee announcing my existence

*Kari Trottier-Whitsitt*

Orb majestic

Magnificent halo of my being

Reciprocate my worship

I carry your torch high and proud

# MOON

## *Heart Reflection*

Full, round mother

Silver night glow

Birth my tides, and rock watery emotion in your crescent cradle

Circular mirror held high against black velvet – reflect soul's
brilliance across dark waters, and light a gentle path

Instinctive knowing

Gut leadership

Follow feeling's tug of truth

Lighthouse knowledge calls all ships in to safe port

Rich, inner world of secrets held

Allow soft light's revealing, and twinkle happy in the night

Ever changing illumination offers no heat, but a cool, silent hand
leads us to morning where her lover has been waiting to warm us

Bring forward her deep beauty and wisdom
of hidden gems into the day

Gift her with gratitude that she may wrap you in loving
arms and sail you safely upon your stormy seas

Sing her siren songs and give her voice

Her reward to you is peace

# MERCURY

## *Witty Orator*

Silver liquid solid — bouncing multiple and sleek about the room

Impossible to grasp or capture

Speedy transformation from one to many

Skid across surfaces — divide and conquer

Messenger, bring me news and knowledge on your way

I know you will not linger

Many are the avenues a mind can explore, with
but little time to decipher each maze

Whisper or shout, write it poetic, or tap out your Morse code

Sing it electric across the wires or ping it back to Earth by satellite

Perhaps you reach me telepathically when
angled to Neptune or the moon

You influence my tongue and decorate my speech —
sharp and witty or sweet as honey

Commute, commune, compute

Communities communicate

Comptroller give commentary of your compact computations

Whet my interest keen and curious — irresistible educator

Teach me the acrobatics of your nimble cerebral circus

# VENUS

## *All Things Nice*

Pink delicacy of love-laced hearts and frosted valentines

Delicious and sweet

Cordial company — the politeness of diplomacy risks no offense

Salutations with beautiful faces of gentle
petals and sugar-coated encounters

She is a smart goddess with a fierce ability to please

Motives wrapped in jewel tones and loveliness
slides smooth across the palate

No doubt she will have her way

Sensual seductress, smooth my jagged ego with
satin fingers and chocolate velvet

Beauty reigns supreme in aesthetic minds, where
chaos and discord have no place

Sweep all cobwebs and shine the silver

Refine crudeness to elegance — cut diamonds
and polished gems sparkle with delight

Symmetry and balance

Equilibrium of fairness spreads joy in the land and all is well

Civilized sensibilities are their own law and order

Exquisite soap bubble waiting to pop

Carefully engage

Love is kind

# MARS

## *The Good Fight*

Roman candles, bottle rockets with red glare

Bursting stars in the air

Glorify war and honor the brave

Troubling archetype, ever present, serves rulers
of nations and all gleaning for power

Its use is not all tainted

Heated combustion pushes effort forward and true courage to protect
or heal — explore, develop and do — lights a fire in the heart of a belly

Action's origin is a hot desire

Moving molecules gaining speed

Expanding gasses need release — beware of the pressure

Offer a valve or endure an explosion

Red hue of intensity, seek an honorable heart
to express your magnificent passion

We need your flame's impetus

Fiery touch — torch of internal drive, ensure success

Curious antagonist, do not stir the bees, but allow honey to be made

Aggressive burst of sure commencement

Get out of the way

Three...two...one...

IGNITE!

# JUPITER

## *Noble Fortune*

Father Christmas, bestower of gifts and happiness

You live large and expansive in our small lives

Position the magnifying glass and show us the bigger picture

Light a truer path with your moral compass and lead us
specific in the way of all good and noble pursuits

Take me on a journey across cultures varying

Open doors of difference where I learn the relativity of values blasting
new awareness in my mind — intricate maze of excelled understanding

Benevolent wisdom

Luck is found by lifting stones and discovered in the search

Enthusiastic explorer of ideas and elastic ideals

Influence active brains to a higher and wider scope of awareness

White light of optimism that beams brilliant upon our faces

Our joy is paying it forward to one another
through good humor, truth and honor

Ethical living

"All for one, and one for all"

Swimming together in a global sea of knowledge

# SATURN

## *Task Master*

Brick walls built high and narrow — structure a
focused pathway of one-way direction

No-nonsense teacher, ruler in hand

Examine, closely, each and every brick — eliminate the unworthy clay

Stay strong of effort, tiring not

Sturdy, well-oiled doors and windows will soon open upon completion

No rushing

A slip on the heavy, uphill push could crush your bones

Painful setback

Limitation and laser-sharp awareness of the
immediate is your only concern

Blinders guide an otherwise distracted workhorse

It is not the time for games or folly

The Little Red Hen is in her heyday, and reward
is plenty and around the bend

One foot in front of other — outside pressure assures your balance

Along a cliff's edge, headmaster's tight grip is comforting

Surrender rebellious notions

Father Time, mark the minutes with responsible discipline

Restrict the urge for recess — school is still in session

You are building your shining autonomy high and proud — a
shatter-proof crystal castle created of your dreams

Applauded perseverance

Your newfound, hard-won authority rings
clear and loud — sure and wise

You arrive a gloriously scarred master

# URANUS

## *High-Voltage Awakener*

"Expect what you can't imagine will happen"

Great liberator — rip the rug out from under my feet

I'm bored of complacency

Too long safe and comfortable — I itch and twitch with erratic drive

Pulverize all walls with electric bolts coming from my
eyes and fingertips — every pore screams freedom

Shake up my sleepy world and stir my waters
muddy — the better to see and sort

Crisis sharpens focus

Perhaps dump all contents and start anew

Rebel — status quo disrupter

Provoke a new order of bohemian utopia

Ahead of your time

Yet unknown mold of independence contains fresh angles
where humanitarian ideals reign primary and clean

Confidently bizarre — quirky master of the cutting edges of evolution

Science and technologies too intricate for common mentality

Lead us not straight, but along interesting and jagged paths — rollercoaster surprises and false floors that fall open to a truer uniqueness of each individual soul

Earthquake realizations of our previous ignorance

Unworthy ideals will drop through the cracks and dissolve molten, while winged enlightenment will rise and innovate a transcendental and brilliant beginning

# NEPTUNE

## *Spirit Knowledge*

Swirling, rich hues of mystery's blue-green,
watercolor world beyond boundaries

Sing your beautiful and haunting song of lucid dreaming

Ruler of mermaids, elves and faerie folk of
nebulous lands — energetic thought forms

Reality knows its many avenues

Truth lies in the gap — spaces alive between
the smallest of seeming particles

Float vivid — knowing without restriction

Imagination's freedom master

Call the mists to sift, cleanse and purify a rough world

Poke holes in theories rigid, that inspiration may leak through

The muse hides in plain sight of softer eyes smiling bright

Fear not your vast enigmatic universe of internal reality
where Higher-Self resides and Spirit knows its way

Answers and questions dance and laugh and dissolve
problems in a joyful soup of soul nourishment

Drink a cup of deep compassion and feel through another's heart

It bleeds the same as yours, as all

Cells of hema, iron in earth, original carbon of star — dust of life

We are all one, split to glorious asunder and
connected by silver, moonlight thread

A heart-thought or prayer plucks a common cord —
we vibrate back together in harmony

Pass through solid walls, or clouds, or illusion — it's all the same

Rearrange material expectation and walk on water

Endless possibility eternally available

The essence of magick is yet undiscovered science

Trust the gut, which requires no cerebral proof

Poetry paints nuance, and we all sigh together...

# PLUTO

## *Death Scythe*

Dark destroyer

Darth Vader of our galaxy

The deep black of your world contrasts light radiant

Hidden secret and hushed by fear, our unsavory
bits hide in dark corners of the psyche

Illusion of containment

Sonic beeps from deep under water sound faint, and
vibration felt in bones affects the whole unknown

Like a floodlight, your unmerciful lever slams white-bright revelation
of naked, squirming, compulsive monsters baring their teeth

Nowhere to escape your ruthless gaze, sorrow
and shame shed tears, and hope is born

Take a closer look

Magnify the warts and lift the virus from its host

Painful extraction

The root runs deep, and healing takes time — scars are
but clean tissue strengthened and stories told true

There is no hero without fall from grace

Stinking rot feeds the submerged seed,
blooming full-petalled magnificence

Excrement makes worthy fuel

Waste not your fetid material, rather, glorify its fertile purpose

Atomic power — plutonium transformation

Metamorphosize a small life larger with newfound wings

Lighten your load with the beauty of death

Rebirth your golden phoenix from ashes time and time again, unending

Dwarf planet of power — no treaties make — but
ignite nuclear war with our covert ignorance

Expose and empower our highest potential for good

# HOUSES

∞

# 1ST HOUSE

## *Initial Impression*

Ascend, our eastern morning glory, and shine my face to the world

Clean window panes allow a peek at my personhood busy
in my house, then offers back my reflection at nightfall

Who am I

You tell me — what do you see

My image gives but a hint

The way my hair curls and my smile dimples —
perhaps Venus resides within

My clothes of flowing fabric and dreamy, green
eyes speaks of Pisces and Neptune

All inhabitants influence my personality, and
I approach life with their gifts

Is there a "Welcome" sign on my door, or
a "Keep Out" mat on the step

Quite apparent, the know-how to greet me

Am I at home often when you come to visit, or journeying afar
with Jupiter freedom or on the winged heels of Mercury

My castle or cottage is uniquely designed and telling

Are you greeted with gates of iron standing heavy in damp mist,
or does sunshine warm happy flowers lining a cobblestoned path

First impressions and book covers bring you initial to my story

Read on

There is more to me beyond the house of the rising Sun

# 2<sup>ND</sup> HOUSE

## *Revered Resources*


Tools and treasures, trinkets and talismans tell of what we value

Materialize inner longing, that we may
stroke the very silk of our dreams

Witnessing our soul's glory and talents with human eyes

Gather all that is yours around

Pen and ink — a writer's instruments...luscious
fabric — a decorator's delight...drums that pound out a
heart's message...archeological specimens building

We are but gods making form of thought

Greed watches from the shadows

Intrinsic value has its own possessive qualities
and also reveals our stories

Trust and love, exhilarating joy, and all things learned to known

True jewels follow us beyond this life

A lesser burden

Living with open palms, making and giving, receiving and sharing

Clay, wood, stone, iron and labor transform in
the artist's hands to inspire and support

Honor with appreciation that beautiful cup tipped to your lips

Truly treasure what is touched by fingers, eyes, ears,
tongue, nasal knowledge, or expansion of feeling

The Earth is our oyster

Live the beauty of your pearl

# 3ᴿᴰ HOUSE

## *Wordliness*

From here to there we walk or roll, and travel familiar paths

Communication is negotiation

Siblings play house or office or school

Practice makes perfect and lion cubs imitate the hunt

"Play nice with the other kids" echoes in adult ears,
whispering, "diplomacy catches more flies"

The Golden Rule, and the ruler's hash marks
segment primary learning manageable

Skills will advance upon this rock, tested peer to peer

Consequence and direction — suspended on the tip of a tongue

Approach is everything in matters of what we say

Sweet-talk the banker and tip the waitress

Treat your fellow cordial

The smaller surround reflects the macro as a raindrop holds the sea

Humanity evolves one encounter at a time, and
the postman will deliver the word

Correspondence written or satellite sent, spoken
or heard, links us one to another

Messages and messengers inform the movement of the day

# 4<sup>TH</sup> HOUSE

## *Motherland*

Hieroglyphic art graces the walls of my would-be cave dwelling

Ancestors naked and raw

Speak to me of my bones

My desire to lie amidst damp stone and mossy green rivulets

A rock fireplace I've built deep within the opening,
surrounded with the gratitude of sheep skin rugs beneath
my feet, and cushy, pillowed luxury for lounging

Juxtapose hard and soft, like mother and father

Sacred sanctuary of my making

I call you home

Central, obsidian water hole for scrying

I look up to floating candles in the air and send
messages on heat waves and smoke

Control room of psychic levers determining intensity of knowing

Somewhere in my genes decodes my witchy heritage

Subverted DNA re-emerges this generation, and my mother shivers

Family resemblance in sepia photo — knowing
eyes look back from the grave

Talents and inclinations carried forward with
wondering why in the heart of the living

Returning from my astral home of sound reality, I enter a modern
kitchen, bare feet on tile floor, and pour myself a cup of coffee

My daughter scribbles a black cat and smiles at the call of a raven

# 5<sup>TH</sup> HOUSE

## *Expressive Extension*

Gather around the heart of my fire

To express is to be seen

Dare I risk your opinion of my creation, so sacred to my core

Pleasure is found in the give and take

With open palms, I present my most personal treasure

Fear lost is confidence gained, and the momentum of play begins

Create beloved children freely, be they art, leadership, song, or soul

All beautiful babies held proudly in loving arms

Out loud, I live my worthy endeavor, and romance all my colors

The sparkling brilliance of my shining attracts a lover to my diamonds

An affair of joy haloed

Honored in celebration of sharing, your smile reflects my gratitude

Let's dance in the sun and seek summer's warmth revealed

My heart glow extends to you

# 6TH HOUSE

## *Work It*

Do better, work harder — gruel out a life

Nagging, wagging finger

Maintain the hive and feed the queen

Oblivious to the effort of mechanistic hum

Sacrificial efficiency

Productivity is a critical god

How do you spend a day

Toil of service is lofty with eyes that lilt to inspiration

Infuse the task with wonder like children play at roles

Every endeavor is but an adventure

Bring whimsy into regimen and ignite a flame beyond match to wax

Stress is illness and health its reverse

Serve creativity, imagination, compassion and joy

The cogs and gears of our day-to-day will
turn smoothly without the squeal

# 7TH HOUSE

## *Other-to-Another*

Extended hand pulls another close

What is in the reach

Secret recognition is a powerful magnet of seeming opposites

Polarities of same composition

Fingers almost touching notice the charge

A sudden tug of truth

The intrigue of other is a one-way mirror that revolves on a central axis

Eliminate the opaque backing and create a
window into each other's world

Mosaic colors fit into wholeness

And individual contribution flavors the blend

Oil and water don't mix, even when sweetness is added

Stir, whip, fold or shake — mix, fuse, and grind

Emulsify the separation

A constancy of union is won

Beyond self is magical territory where secret gardens
bloom and weather is ever-changing

Add a verse to my song, and interest my story anew

One plus one intrigues quantum mathematicians

Beware toxic combinations clouded in sickly emissions

Enemies do serve a purpose, and poisons can be medicine

Be careful in the tasting

Trust the gut before the tongue

Inclination determines the pairing

# 8TH HOUSE

## Obsessive Transcendence

Le petit mort – speak to me of letting go

Sighs of ecstasy in sweet release

I surrender my hold to feigned sanity and surface transcendent

Uneasy monsters squint through enlightenment's bright white

Remnants of perceived sin still dripping from the newborn perspective

Rebirth these soiled, putrid thoughts and habits –
old notions chained captive to self-loathing

Secret wounds and hidden scars

Beauty, trembling, has awaited her unearthing

Peering deeply into the kaleidoscope of another's eyes,
we're captured in blended merging of rich color

Sharing resources of various hues that shine
together a new color entirely

I sacrifice control to transform your bounty into
mine and play out your legacy for all time

Use me as you will and support my very existence

I empower you to feed my future, and my
creations will shine your glory

Inheritance rolls new stones, altering a river's course

Deep catacombs hold your locked vault of
treasures – my loyalty is the key

Exalted state of communion – the yin and yang of interdependence

Power teaches me its proper use, and my naked
vulnerability glows opulent with gratitude

# 9ᵀᴴ HOUSE

## *Traveling Tunes*

Take to the road, wandering gypsy

Seeker of freedom

New frontiers glow golden on the distant horizon, luring
the intelligence of the human spirit forward

Tidbits of varied truths

Snaggles of facts attach to questioning
brains, evolving a matrix of belief

Dancing theories and opinions — like jingling coins on
scarf around waist, sing the knowledge of the hips

Gather round foreign tables and tip your
cup to ideas and exotic thought

Become drunk on possibility — creating new cerebral
avenues that feed a broadening mind

Personal religion

Our stories that change filters as we experience
deep mystery's knowledge firsthand

Shoot your arrow straight for the sun and follow its course
to enlightenment, sharpening your aim with each failure

Mistakes are diamonds in your crown — every wrong
turn's adventure offering yet new questions

Life is a benevolent playground of inspiration

Joyful ideals feed the spirit giving meaning to our existence

Shining smile of optimism, lead us carefree into discovery of
a better world, where each voice sings true their song

# 10TH HOUSE

## *On High*

Quarry stone built solid into castle walls

Overlook the valley below

Soak in the warmth of the sun — no obstruction on high

Reign your life supreme in its pinnacle and claim your authority

Rulership of your blood's vocation

The higher calling that vibrates your bones

High noon of development — a standoff with childhood

Who will win the dual

Talents mastered offer the most, and acclaim
shouts maximum glory and strength

Take the highest qualities and apply them here

The ones you want written on your gravestone

What are we to give others but the best of ourselves

Weave the shining gold and diamond clarity into your cloth

Be it presidential or exaltation in service

Best intention leads to worthy application where all benefit

We are queens or kings of our own soul's
lands and authors of our own stories

Hero or Villain — Sage or Fool

All interesting tales

Reputation will build our raft that floats or
sinks on the river of humanity

Top of your game — all eyes watching

What of your merits will you gift us

# 11<sup>TH</sup> HOUSE

## *Collective*

Countless leaves collect chlorophyll that feeds
the tree, and fish swim in schools

Many are more and effort is less when hands and minds work together

Kindred sister, brother, unite in common cause
and lift humanity a rung or two

The reverberation of a single heartbeat
activates those of shared rhythm

Mutual bleeding for goodness is a blood-letting our world requires

Closer to sanity and grace as we recognize our divinity in one another

A charge ignites motion for change

Stimulate masses to group cohesive unions of effectual thought

Mental and extra-sensory with the ability
to quantum leap without regard

Something in the core knowledge of me attaches to the core
knowledge of you, then another, and we make history

Shouts of indignation hang sharp in the air, freshly
released, creating awareness for new eyes

Like time folded on itself, we can touch our
very future in this moment together

The hand of a friend is warm with encouragement
and welcomes zany play

Point of discovery where blended creativities form solid a solution

Resonance and tuning forks and geometric patterns in nature

A commonality of knowing something essential

And the choir sings Hallelujah in unison

# 12<sup>TH</sup> HOUSE

## *Netherland*

Secret knowing, like the silence of empty
black space, comforts my existence

I slip into your arms so easily

Whispered instruction caught in dreams or waking
trance, light a misty path before me

Keep the eyes soft and the mind boundless
as a starry night on a mountain top

Moving through the world — feet barely touching the earth

Like a song that hangs on the edge of thought

Nothing vigorous — only languid reaching
toward a softly glowing unknown

A single drop of water feels every pulse of
the ocean and ripples its truth

Compassion sponge of oneness dripping empathy

Water the earth with our tears filtered through love

Universality is endless and incomprehensible —
territory of the soul, where brain is no master

Denouncement of rulership by visionaries and mystics

Realm of divination

Show a way through the mist and fog of ethereal
where answers await a worthy question

Blue-green mosaic of liquid glass

Step through the mirror to other worlds, parallel
and altered states of your being

Limitless realities exist and revealed only to the imaginative

Delegates of awareness, inspire us wise

Look into the green eyes of Neptune and sail safely the spirit, home

# ELEMENTS

∞

# FIRE

## *Inspiration*

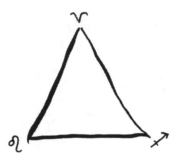

Fireball core

Melt your way to the surface in liquid heat to cooling
glass, or explode as Pele's fury creating islands rising

Flash — Jump — Act

Leap rivers and spark a flame

Ravage a change and birth a pine forest to grace the world

Red hair of fiery blood, scream out a fierce song

And pound a wild heart's rhythm as we stomp our feet in cadence

Native dance, frenzied rave, or soldier's march

Big — Bold — Loud

Fight

Punch a fist of freedom through walls built to restrain and control

Who will heat the lazy water to boiling

Useful as pressurized steam turning engines of
mechanistic progress or destruction

Fire in the belly transforms a static muse to
the creative instability of active

Suffer the force that plays out primal potency in the birth of a soul

Blow torch burning pain of crowning

Becomes glory wrapped in Mother's arms

Victory over death

Protective dragon to this small life — for life — maternal firepower

Stars in eyes and hearts of beasts and saints
ignite the night with passion

I stare into the glowing embers' mesmerizing, red-velvet softness
of hell-fire, and am lead through a white-hot tunnel

Origin of spirit is found

# EARTH

## *Execution*

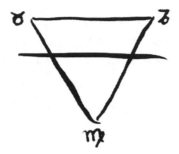

Mud and guts and stone and bones

Iron and carbon of bursting star

Dust made planet and people and all glorious manner of inhabitants

Speeding molecules spinning create the grand illusion of solid

Hand on smooth glass leaves oily vapor print
behind — evidence of material reality

Physical senses capture treasured moments of
form's beauty in cut and polished gem

Or olfactory pleasure gifted from a sun-kissed rose petal

Resources soak our cells in delight of greens
and golds and rich dark soil

And crude black oil keeps all cogs moving

Splash wildly in river's roaring laughter, and
embrace every gift of sustenance

Bodies beautiful and gleaming

Muscles move mountains and make love rise to the occasion

Warmest of woods

I lie wet-refreshed on the dock and drink in the
aroma of your sap in the heat of the day

Salt-of-the-earth renders one legitimate

Realm of the work horse

Mold clay with strong hands and build cities brick by brick

Steady and methodical beneath a loving sun

Effort, made currency, records a certain worth on a spreadsheet

Account balance worthless beyond the grave –
trivial beyond a body's need

But a body's need directs the day

While spirit remains manifest

# AIR

## *Deliberation*

Open all windows and doors, and allow me free passage

Boxed in air is trapped and stale and stinks of lingering pain

Stone not my butterfly thoughts that lightly touch and flit curious
around a closed mind, dangerous with its heavy hand

Leaves freely and individually dance with the
breeze, and I inhale with gratitude

Clouds shapeshift with moving currents and speak to our imaginations —
stimulus to inventors, creators and all provoked by cerebral play

Teeters and totters and tinkers tick out a rhythmic
code — master is the mind of matter

Crystal clarity is mental serenity and insight expresses a
sigh of knowledge in a brilliant flow of ink or tongue

Lightly be burden free with gauzy wings uplifting

Gather force in cyclone spin to break our chains and bondage

Blow it all away to open

Clear skies of eternal blue

# WATER

## *Emotion*

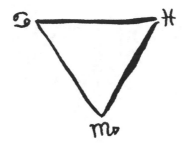

Blood knowledge, fill my veins and I will divine your message

Fluid intuition – pervasive and turgid as cohesive droplets made mist

Form to the container – riverbanks, coastal cliffs, or sacred cauldron

With gulping thirst, I drink of deep, wine-red vintage
secrets and feel the agony of truth begging for breath

The moon spills a rippling path across the lake and I glide on water

I stare at the glassy, still surface, and my eyes soften
and mind unlocks entrances to unseen worlds

Scry the existence all around and within,
and greet mythical messengers

Water befriends electricity – conducting energy
of past, present and changing forms

The songs of whales surely resonate with the beauty of Calla Lily

All space between, pregnant with possibility

Memory can strike a cord and pool tears in
our eyes – high tide of the heart

Storm clouds gather the probability of a hurricane eminent

Evoke nature's power of fluid force and clear your land anew

Destroy remnants of suffering along dissolved borders of previous
obstruction, and breathe fresh the negative ions uplifting

Ride the waves of your glorious surf and
arrive exhilarated upon the shore

# QUALITIES

∞

# CARDINAL

## *Start*

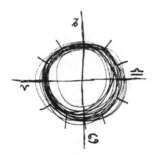

Soldier at the ready, pawn of chessboard —
Someone must be first to move

Others rely on the sure step forward

Reigns in hand, lead us to water

First step on the moon, a pioneer footprints
our future with more than hope

Initiate inertia's death by enterprise and reap
the inheritance locked therein

Sunrise opens sleepy eyes refreshed by night's
solitude, and the day is set in motion

Babies know what it takes to get fed, and
the lover's kiss ignites a response

Commencement introduces momentum's rolling
thunder with initial strike of energy

Begin

# FIXED

## *Stay*

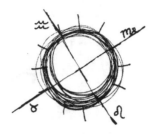

Steady fulcrum — Center of balance

Peace resides in stillness

Unchanging security of sameness, your
strong walls protect the status quo

Impenetrable, unmoving — you cannot tip the iron bull

Solid, heavy, fierce stability of stubborn demeanor —
guard at the gate — bouncer at the bar

The one you want on your side

Loyalty is eternal stick-with-it

A stance taken

Do not disturb a sleeping lion

Territories will make known their boundaries, and
the bounty within locked and vaulted

It takes a knowing key to shift a precise matrix
to its new and higher groundedness

Roots will again take hold

# MUTABLE

## *Shapeshift*

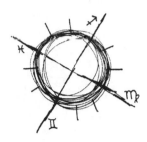

Fluid molds to its container and uses substance as support

Adaptability is the higher skill and survival requires changing our colors

Wishy-washy reputation speaks to a certain
intelligence – The smarts of flow and change

Chameleon awareness of brown on brown and when in Rome...

Keen attention to intuit crucial nuance establishes
the next move, and we live another day

Or make a quick escape

Invisibility is a super-power

Taste all influence of environment and you'll know which spice to add

Stir the air widdershins to counter and confuse

Reset the resonance, they'll never know what happened

Seeming compliance strokes authority's need to
take care, and the next meal is supplied

Who is really in charge

The water or the riverbank

# OVERVIEW

∞

# COSMOS CALLING

## *Divine Influence*

Moving bodies encircle the Sun, like skyclad
dancers around a sacred bonfire

Goddesses and gods make nice or play war in
an ever-expanding spiral overhead

Energy flows, balances, connects or repels — We are not unaffected

The mere lift of a butterfly's wing alters the whole, like
spinning planet's massive gravitas of definitive pull

Unseen influence felt at heart and bone of similar substance
turns the day a particular way, and opportunity is at hand

Take the cue and act out your part

The problem holds the interest of the audience,
and resolution is sweet or sorrowful

Who are the players on your personal stage,
and which god will appear today

Integrate the many to harmonious, or at least
create allies of varying proclivities within

Alter your sauce accordingly

Sweet and salty or hot and savory

Will others complement or clash with your unique flavor

Opposites attract and polarities have power

But realize the two sides of one coin are made of the same material

Perspective is the difference

Make love with all internal players and
avoid schizophrenic fragmentation

Life after life of purposeful passion play

Souls dance among the stars singing songs of Glory Hallelujah

The curtain falls

Take a bow

# ASTROLOGY KEY

## *Signs = "How"- Who and How We Are*

| ARIES | TAURUS | GEMINI |
|---|---|---|
| **Mar 21-Apr 20** | **Apr 21-May 21** | **May 22-June 21** |
| **Mars Ruler** | **Venus Ruler** | **Mercury Ruler** |
| **Fire/Cardinal/1ˢᵗ House Natural** | **Earth/Fixed/2ⁿᵈ House Natural** | **Air/Mutable/3ʳᵈ House Natural** |
| Enthusiastic, Energetic and Adventurous | Patient and Long-Suffering | Quick-witted and Intellectual |
| Pioneering and Brave | Sensual and Appreciative | Highly Communicative |
| Highly Confident | Determined and Unbending | Multi-tasking and Multi-focused |
| Dynamic and Self-Oriented | Self-Sufficient and Capable | Quick-thinker and Light-hearted |
| Quick, Hot Temper | Slow-paced and Stubborn | Outgoing and Fun |
| Aggressive and Impatient | Steady, Talented, and Kind | Curious and Clever |
| Impulsive and Youthful Warrior | Self-indulgent and Greedy | Non-committal and Unreliable Communicator |
| | Builder | |

| CANCER | LEO | VIRGO |
|---|---|---|
| June 22-July 22 | July 23-Aug 21 | Aug 22-Sep 23 |
| Moon Ruler | Sun Ruler | Mercury Ruler |
| Water/Cardinal/4th House Natural | Fire/Fixed/5th House Natural | Earth/Mutable/6th House Natural |
| Emotional and Caring | Enthusiastic and Warmhearted | Reliable and Modest |
| Intuitive and Imaginative | Creative and Generous | Detailed and Meticulous |
| Dependable and Loyal | Faithful and Protective | Practical and Helpful |
| Protective and Cautious | Proud and Patronizing | Analytical and Perfectionistic |
| Changeable and Moody | Charismatic and Happy | Earthy and Fastidious |
| Oversensitive and Self-pitying | Attention-seeking and Self-confident | Overcritical and Harsh |
| Clinging to the Past and Security-oriented | Dogmatic and Bossy | Conservative and Discriminating |
| Caregiver | Performer | Service to Other |

| LIBRA | SCORPIO | SAGITTARIUS |
|---|---|---|
| **Sep 24-Oct 23** | **Oct 24-Nov 22** | **Nov 23-Dec 22** |
| **Venus Ruler** | **Pluto Ruler** | **Jupiter Ruler** |
| **Air/Cardinal/7th House Natural** | **Water/Fixed/8th House Natural** | **Fire/Mutable/9th House Natural** |
| Polite and Diplomatic | Determined and Resourceful | Optimistic and Freedom-loving |
| Romantic and Caring | Emotional, Intuitive, and Melding | Good-natured and Humorous |
| Charming and Sociable | Powerful and Passionate | Honest and Straightforward |
| Fair and Peace-loving | Sexual and Magnetic | Intellectual and Philosophical |
| Indecisive and Open-minded | Jealous and Resentful | Blindly Optimistic and Carefree |
| Superficial and Easily Influenced | Compulsive and Obsessive | Open-minded and Broad thinking |
| Flirtatious and Refined | Secretive, Suspicious, Manipulative | Tactless and Restless |
| Sociable | Transformative | Generous of spirit |

| CAPRICORN | AQUARIUS | PISCES |
|---|---|---|
| **Dec 23-Jan 20** | **Jan 21-Feb 19** | **Feb 20-Mar 20** |
| **Saturn Ruler** | **Uranus Ruler** | **Neptune Ruler** |
| **Earth/Cardinal/10th House Natural** | **Air/Fixed/11th House Natural** | **Water/Mutable/12th House Natural** |
| Practical and Serious | Friendly and Humanitarian | Imaginative and Highly Sensitive |
| Ambitious and Disciplined | Quirky and Detached | Compassionate and Spiritual |
| Responsible and Careful | Original and Inventive | Selfless and Other-worldly |
| Task Oriented and Reserved | Highly Independent and Intellectual | Intuitive and Empathetic |
| Capable and Successful | Insightful and Individualistic | Artistic and Creative |
| Pessimistic and Unimaginative | Unconventional and Unemotional | Escapist and Idealistic |
| Inhibited and Distrusting | Unpredictable and Contrary | Secretive and Vague |
| Authoritarian | Free-thinker | Mystical |

# ASTROLOGICAL KEY

## *Planets = "What" — What Part of Our Personality are We Talking About*

**Planets**

| SUN | MOON | MERCURY |
|---|---|---|
| Ego, conscious mind, creative life force, aspirations, inner self, will, Father | Emotional nature, deepest personal needs, Mother, unconscious, emoting | How we think, communication style, intellect, coordination of ideas, sensory information, day-to-day expression |
| **VENUS** | **MARS** | **JUPITER** |
| How we relate with others one-on-one, what we like, talents, resources, beauty, romantic attraction, leisure | Action, energy, drive, sexual desire, anger expressed, 1$^{st}$ instinct to act | Insight through knowledge, expansion of purpose, optimism, law, philosophy |
| **SATURN** | **URANUS** | **NEPTUNE** |
| Restriction, limitation, structure, boundaries, responsibility, commitment, authority | Where we are original, uniqueness, upheaval, change, genius/brilliance, invention, generational change | Intuition, psychic sensitivity, dreams, subconscious, spirituality, compassion, oneness, imagination |

| PLUTO Letting go, endings and beginnings, rebirth, transformation, power and control | | |
|---|---|---|

## Houses

*Houses = "Where"—What area of Life (like the purpose of a room in your house)*

| 1ST HOUSE | 2ND HOUSE | 3RD HOUSE |
|---|---|---|
| Self, Ascendant, Personality, Natural Demeanor, First Impression | Personal Resources, Finances, Talents, Our Personal Assets, What We Value | Immediate Surroundings, K-12 Education, Communications, Siblings, Short Travel, Day-To-Day Encounters |
| 4TH HOUSE | 5TH HOUSE | 6TH HOUSE |
| Home, Family, History/ Ancestry, Childhood And Emotions, Mother Or Father | Children, Creative Expressions, Risk-Taking/Gambling, Recreation, Love Affairs, Self-Expression, Pleasure | Service To Others, Health, Daily Work, Everyday Life, Peers At Work |
| 7th HOUSE | 8th HOUSE | 9th HOUSE |
| Others, One-On-One Relationship, Marriage, Associations, Contracts, Open Enemies, Descendant | Transformation, Sex, Death, Birth, Other People's Resources, Passions And Crises | Travel, Higher Education, Foreign Matters, Higher and Abstract Concepts, Philosophical Outlook |

| 10<sup>th</sup> HOUSE | 11<sup>th</sup> HOUSE | 12 HOUSE |
|---|---|---|
| Career/Vocation, Social Elevation, Reputation, Authority, Ambition and Achievement | Friends, Groups and Group Activities, Kindred People, Common Causes, Humanitarian Issues | Spirituality, Subconscious, Inner Life, Dreams, Hidden Enemies, Hidden Aspects of Self, Solitude, Places of Confinement, The Unseen |

## Elements

*Elements = "The Nature of"*

| FIRE | EARTH | AIR | WATER |
|---|---|---|---|
| Energy, Heat, Flair, Action, Self-Expression, Inspiring | Manifestation, Solidity, Touch, Grounded, Creating, Physicality, Practicality | Perception, Insight, Ideation, Cerebral Expression, Thought | Emotional, Intuitive, Feeling, Responsive, Empathy |

## Qualities

*Qualities = "Our Approach To" – How We Navigate*

| CARDINAL | FIXED | MUTABLE |
|---|---|---|
| Initiation of Energy, Principal of Action | Solidity of Purpose, Concrete, Steadfast, Immovable | Flexible and Adaptable, Fluid, Changing, Spiraling |

# ABOUT THE AUTHOR

Kari Trottier-Whitsitt is Taurus Sun with Pisces Moon and Pisces Rising. Her chart ruler is Neptune in Scorpio. Kari is a new author who has found her wings in expressing her inner language of poetry. Her debut volume, *Charted Territories: Astrology in Poetry* reflects her avid knowledge of the subject matter as well as highlights her skillful use of nuance and subtlety. Kari is a practicing astrologer and metaphysician of over forty years and gives consultations/readings under her business name of "The Witch Doctor." With a lifelong interest in all things mysterious and scientific, she has investigated many fields of science, metaphysics, and magick (which she refers to as quantum physics applied). She has studied astrology since the age of thirteen and discovered a passionate calling for helping others with self-discovery and personal transformation through the integration of their most authentic selves. After many years of writing, Kari has found *her* most authentic voice in poetry which beautifully reflects her mode of thinking and being in the world. She has many current books up her sleeve and has definitely found her home in the poetry genre. Kari lives in her hometown of Boise, Idaho with her wife and 2 cats. You can contact Kari at mailto:kariwhitsitt@msn.com. Also, check out Kari's website at: http://kariwhitsitt.wix.com/the-poet and *The Witchdoctor* FB page at https://www.facebook.com/The-Witch-Doctor-1591269024451072/

Printed in the United States
By Bookmasters